TEMPUS
Oral History
SERIES

BARNET
voices

Public transport played a significant part in shaping the way of life of most Barnet citizens. By 1908, for example, motor buses such as this one ran every 12 minutes (at 12 miles per hour) from North Finchley to Oxford Circus.

TEMPUS
Oral History
SERIES

BARNET
voices

Compiled by
Percy Reboul

TEMPUS

First published 1999
Copyright © Percy Reboul, 1999

Tempus Publishing Limited
The Mill, Brimscombe Port,
Stroud, Gloucestershire, GL5 2QG

ISBN 0 7524 1562 X

Typesetting and origination by
Tempus Publishing Limited
Printed in Great Britain by
Midway Clark Printing, Wiltshire

Barnet Fair was an annual event looked forward to by most (but not all) sections of the population. The fair began in the sixteenth century and continues, albeit much altered, to this day. When this photograph was taken, in the 1920s, much of the machinery was powered by steam.

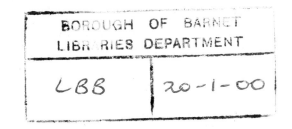
CONTENTS

This delightful family group, Mrs Sutton and her two children, were photographed at the turn of the century by James Barber, a talented local photographer. The family lived in one of the fine houses in Parson Street, Hendon.

Royal visits were occasions to be remembered and all were enthusiastically supported. Here, the Duke of York, later to become George VI, is visiting the Standard Telephone & Cable Company in New Southgate in 1934.

INTRODUCTION

It is only in recent times that we have begun to value, and take steps to preserve, the memories and experiences of ordinary people. Part of the reason for this is the ready availability of easy-to-operate sound recording equipment but part is also due to families and individuals keeness to preserve and pass on to future generations, information about their own background and experience. The family bore has sometimes become the centre of attention – however briefly.

This collection of 'tales' is based on a series of tape recordings made in the late 1970s and 1980s. They have two things in common: first, all the subjects were elderly, born and raised in the late nineteenth and early twentieth centuries. Secondly, all were living in what is today's London Borough of Barnet.

At the turn of the century, the borough itself comprised a number of small rural and urban districts whose main economy was agriculture. The total population in 1901 was a mere 76,000 – today it is well over 300,000. As the tales graphically reveal, however, change was in the air. It had started dramatically around the middle of the nineteenth century, with the coming of the railways. Now further fruits of Victorian and Edwardian science and technology were about to be exploited: wireless telegraphy, the telephone, the aeroplane, motor cars, photography – the list is formidable. Even the horse, for centuries the main motive power, was about to be replaced, albeit gradually, by the wonders of electric power and the internal combustion engine.

Family events such as weddings are often remembered in detail by older people. Such occasion were frequently recorded by local photographers and everyone concerned dressed in their Sunday best for the event. Seen here are the Catchpole and Prockter families celebrating a christening in 1896 outside their home in Whetstone's High Road.

One such development provides the key to some of the changes hinted at in these stories: the coming of cheap, reliable and frequent public transport. The electric tram and the mechanically propelled bus (also, later, the Underground) enabled our area to be linked to most parts of London and other centres of work. For many people, almost for the first time, the poor pay and limited prospects offered by local farming and service industries were to become things of the past. In short, it was now possible to live in the country and commute to the city – a major factor in the huge population increases of later years.

Transcribing an hour-long tape into a thousand words or so requires some sacrifices. I am mindful of two of the current schools of thought: one which insists that nothing should be added or subtracted to what has been said, even down to the 'ums and ahs', and the other which recognizes the unstructured nature of casual conversation and allows for a certain amount of editing. In the interest of a 'good read' I have tended towards the latter school whilst in every case taking care to preserve the spirit and truth of the original. The photographs, in most cases, are from my own collection but I am indebted to the staff of the London Borough of Barnet Archive and Local Studies Department who filled in certain gaps and were, as ever, helpful in so many ways. Finally, and most importantly, my thanks go to the shades of all those delightful people who gave of their time to share their memories. Their kindness and co-operation was an inspiration.

Percy Reboul
Hendon, July 1999

CHAPTER 1

The Refugee's Tale

The six Schuricht boys photographed just before 1914. Their father was killed in the early days of the First World War. Hans Schuricht, the subject of our tale, is on the extreme left.

Hans Schuricht's mother, who overcame great odds to raise her six children during and after the war.

I was born in December 1905 in Berlin. My father was an orphan and my mother came from a farmworker's family who went into service in what is today Poland. There were six boys in our family: I was the eldest. My father was killed in the early days of the war in 1915 when I was nine. Because there were six sons, a Professor Wolf took an interest in us. He had lost a son and was the author of historical romantic novels and he arranged for my mother and us to be moved to what was called a 'soldiers' settlement' in a small town near the River Oder. My mother had a small widow's pension but it was not big enough. She couldn't earn money because there was no work.

We moved back to Berlin. We literally had nothing to eat and my mother was always ill but she worked hard by delivering newspapers and being a caretaker. When you are nine you don't think of whether things are hard or not as long as you get a stulle (a slice of bread with sugar on it). I don't know how my mother did it. It's beyond belief. She worked for other people, cleaned houses and I remember on a number of occasions she helped out at weddings because she came home with all kinds of cakes – they were feast days! Above all, she managed to get my brothers good jobs with well-known firms such as Siemens. When I was fourteen, I worked as a clerk in a firm making buckles and metal objects. I was paid a pittance of £1 a week for three years when you were automatically thrown out to make way for another unemployed person.

In 1922, I was unemployed and living with a girl who later became my wife. I got unemployment pay and it was the loveliest time we ever had. We had second-hand bikes and lived in a nudist colony about thirty miles from Berlin with a beautiful secluded lake where we had a tent. We were all left-wingers. My future wife Ella and I joined the Socialist Workers' Party in 1931 and became members of a trade union. We went three times a week to evening school to study many subjects. Hitler came to power shortly after and then it started. He had an unbelievable following. The middle classes were all for him because they had lost everything due to the inflation; their savings had dwindled and there was enormous unemployment. The working classes joined partly out of conviction, partly because others had joined. They didn't know what they had let themselves in for – that I grant. We were lucky enough to know and look behind the scene.

We were working for our political party in our section of Berlin and, in December 1933, went for a holiday on a little farm on the Czech-German border. A friend of ours turned up after looking for us for three days and told us we couldn't come back because they had searched and sealed our room and found political material. We had no money and a useless return ticket so we walked towards Prague where we found friends who had escaped. Ella had earlier worked as an au pair in Surbiton in England for a family called Friedlander, so we walked to Paris, where I stayed,

Part of old Berlin, just before the war.

and Ella went to England for three weeks. It was very difficult to get into England in 1934 but our English friends invited us to come to the royal wedding of Princess Marina – which was an excuse. The Party gave us money and tickets and we were let in.

At Surbiton, my miserable life began! I couldn't speak English. I couldn't even understand the milkman or the postman. We kept house for our friends and bit by bit settled down. I went to college to learn English and elocution. One day, someone suggested that I start my own business. I had applied three times for a work permit and was turned down each time but was told by the Home Office that there would be no objection if I started my own business. I started with 5s and went into the duplicating business. Through a friend I borrowed the Labour Party's duplicator when I had a job to do. My God! My English! But bit by bit I worked day and night for about £5 a month. One day, Mr Goldstein of Gestetner offered me a splendid second-hand machine for £70 and I paid that off promptly. I taught myself what quality is. My old samples show our work was good – dark, sharply cut and everything you could wish for. By 1938, I had reached the stage where I could go out and buy my own typewriter – I still have it.

Left-wing political parties were strong in Germany immediately after the war. This 1929 photograph shows a party of Welsh miners on a visit to Berlin. The young Schurichts are seated third and fifth from the left.

Internment

It was obvious in 1938 that there would be a war. I could not understand that everywhere you looked there were people who just did not want to know that war was coming and I was even accused of warmongering. People did not believe me when I spoke about what was going on outside England because they were terribly insular. We just waited. We couldn't do anything.

When war was declared, we were living in a posh neighbourhood near Surbiton. We never had any trouble with local people but we had to appear before a tribunal of very nice lay people who screened us and we were entered as aliens. We could prove we were political refugees and got through with flying colours. We were given ration and identity cards but this did not stop them from interning me in the end.

One morning in June 1940, just before Dunkirk, two detectives came and wanted to take me away for internment. We were not prepared for it and asked them to have a cup of tea. Then one of them said they had to go to Chessington Zoo and offered to collect me later – they did not want my wife. By the time they returned I was packed. They took me, with other people, by car to Kempton Park racecourse and put us under the grandstand but the next day we were put in a special train guarded by soldiers and taken to Huyton, Liverpool. There, we were given blankets and a straw palliasse and marched into blocks of flats. We were there several weeks and were well treated, with good food.

Ella and Hans Schuricht around the time Hitler became Chancellor of Germany in 1933.

We were then transferred to a hotel in Douglas on the Isle of Man. The journey was terrible. Outside [the hotel] was a barbed-wire fence with a soldier at the entrance. Here, we were left to our own devices. There were big army tents and we had our meals there. The food, which was cooked in the open, was good. Army papers and envelopes were provided to write home but all letters were censored and it took weeks before it reached them and before they replied.

In the camp, after a short time when everything was organized, they started a nice little industry. Gifted people did sketches on postcard size paper and sold them to earn money. There was an issue of army boots to those who could prove

13

that their shoes were worn out. The man running this (he was an Austrian I think) said I could wait because my shoes were not too bad. He had the most beautiful pair of army boots I have ever seen! So I walked into his room when he wasn't there and took his – that's how things were done. I had to muddy the boots so that he couldn't recognize them.

We had officially arranged concerts and there were two men, Ravicz and Landauer, pianists, who managed to get a grand piano. They were terrible snobs. Later on, all kinds of classes were

set up. There was a man who gave lectures on philosophy, another on architecture and all kinds of things. Some of the officers were retired teachers and one of them formed a group of what he called 'hand-picked internees' and arranged long walks for them around Douglas. I was very grateful.

No-one tried to escape, but we talked about it and made certain preparations in case the Germans came. We found a large piece of timber that could be used as a battering ram but where would we have gone? The worry affected some people terribly and there were suicides by poor devils who had had a hard time in Germany and lived on their nerves. We were not regimented in any way and I can remember only one time when there was a count of people. The worst thing was the boredom.

After six months or so I was released and given a ticket to travel to London. I felt that there was no justification for my internment.

Hans Schuricht
Recorded September 1981

Second World War aliens, mainly from Germany and Austria, were interned in Liverpool and the Isle of Man. To earn money, many of the talented artists in the camps drew portraits such as this one.

14

CHAPTER 2
The Railwayman's Tale

A Metropolitan train at night (artist: Joe James).

Rayner's Lane Halt in the 1920s. The wooden platforms were occasionally set on fire by carelessly discarded cigarette ends.

I'm sixty-eight years of age next June [Ed.: born in 1914] and I was born in Willesden, Middlesex. My father was a railwayman. He was a train driver on the Metropolitan Railway driving electric locomotives and he was a senior driver. They were called 'fluffylinks' because they had a special rota of duties which made other train drivers look upon them as being apart and favoured. My father opened the Stanmore branch in 1932. He drove the first train with Lord Abercrombie in the cab. I remember being at the cinema at that time and seeing the newsreel which showed the opening of the line and when the camera was in the cab and swung to the driver, I stood up and shouted 'That's my dad!'

We were a close family and I had a happy childhood. My brother was on the railway. He started in 1926 and

ended up as a District Inspector. My dad's mother was the ladies' waiting room attendant at Baker Street for sixteen years. In her days the stationmaster wore a top hat.

I was destined for the railways. When I was fourteen I went to Baker Street for an interview and was accepted after a medical. I started as a parcel boy in the Baker Street Parcels Office working two shifts, 7 a.m. to 3 p.m. and 3 p.m. to 11 p.m. This involved sitting on the back of a horse-drawn parcel van to protect the back from thieves and to make deliveries. We collected and delivered in the West End. The horses were well groomed and looked after. Every year we entered the Easter Horse Parade in Regent's Park and I can't recollect any year when we didn't get a first prize. I worked a 48-hour week for 16s a week. My mother was given 12s

16

and I had to put 2s in the Metropolitan Railway Providence savings bank (a family tradition) and the other 2s was my pocket money.

I was two and a half years in the department and I got bored with it, so in 1930 I went as a junior porter to Eastcote station which was a very rural station surrounded by fields. Purdy's, the gun people, had a shooting ground in the area and well-to-do people came down to Eastcote with their rifles and guns in beautiful cases. As a porter, you offered to carry their guns up the slope (there were no stairs then) and sometimes you'd get a penny or twopence tip, which was welcome. The Sunday school outings, if they didn't make for Hadley Woods, made for Eastcote where Bayliss's had a pavilion and fun fair. Special trains came down from Hammersmith carrying mostly poor children and the District Line used to run at least eight (and sometimes sixteen) specials for the children.

My job was to keep the station clean, wash the signals which were oil-lit in those days (a filled lamp, incidentally, burnt for three days), attend the trains and collect tickets on the down side. The Stationmaster, based at Ruislip, looked after a group of stations and came once a day to inspect things. He could sack you.

A rural station like Eastcote was dead at night and girls called in at the station and romances were always going on. Girl passengers, on a Sunday evening, brought food down to cook on our stove and we'd have a meal going knowing full well that no one would call in the evening. The local police constable also used to call in for a cup of

Joe James after his accident, working in the control office of the Circle and Metropolitan lines at Baker Street, 1954.

Joe James in retirement at his house in Totteridge Lane, Whetstone.

tea, a smoke and a chat. It was a lovely life that doesn't exist on the railways today.

Later, I became a booking porter at Rayner's Lane. At that time the Piccadilly trains were by now coming through. In the London area, the signals were electric: out in the country they were oil-lit and often got blown out, which the Piccadilly drivers found difficult to accept. One night, in March 1934, a heavy gale was blowing and all four signals at the gas works sidings were blown out and the Piccadilly drivers refused to come down unless the lights were lit. So I had to down tools, lock up the station, and go and relight them. I walked up to the viaduct which was a horrible place to walk in the pitch black because cables ran on the side walls and you had to walk on the tracks. I knew the lamps would never stay alight in this wind and rain was sheeting across. I had

to climb up a steel ladder into the crow's nest and relight the lamps and then I walked up to where the road branches off into the gasworks. The sleepers were oily and greasy and I must have slipped, hitting my head and I don't remember anything until I woke up on the track. My left leg was off and my other badly smashed in sixty places and turned back to front. The only fortunate thing was that when my leg was severed it hit the trip and operated the train's emergency brakes. I'm lying there; I couldn't get my wind. My head was on the rail of the track and I couldn't move or speak. I could hear the driver talking to the guard on the internal telephone and the guard then opened his door – I was just beneath him – and he looked down… They stopped a train coming in the other direction (which would have taken my head off) with a hand lamp.

I had done first aid with the Metropolitan Railway and I knew I was going because blood was pumping out. I whispered to the guard to get a piece of string to make a tourniquet and a passenger pushed a piece of string through the ventilator window. I eventually finished up in Harrow hospital. My father came down, poor old bloke, and came into the side ward where I was lying waiting for a specialist to arrive. I said to him 'There's some excess fare in my pocket, Dad, make sure that it's paid in.' He always remarked on that. Even as I was, the railway came first. The things that you do. I was nineteen at the time. They didn't find my foot until next day. One of the lamp porters brought it up, his name was Brasier and he always had a dew-drop on the end of his nose. He sat beside me and said 'I've brought your foot in, Joe!'

Joseph James
Recorded April 1982

CHAPTER 3
The Mayor's Tale

East End Road in the early years of the twentieth century.

A page from a publicity brochure advertising newly built houses in Friern Watch Avenue.

I came to Finchley in 1912. I had a cousin who worked in the chemical industry in the East End. He lived in Finchley and he and I were good friends and we decided to share lodgings off East End Road. Opposite us was Killingbeck, the bakers, and it used to amuse me when people took their joints of meat (and, at Christmas time, turkeys) into his shop to be cooked.

I was working for an estate developer, Newcombe Estates Limited, whose office was Friern Watch House. Friern Watch was a lovely country estate then, with cattle still breeding there; the house was eventually sold to the local authorities. A general manager and myself were the only two people employed and our job was to lay out and mark out the sites of the new estate. The manager was often away and I would be left alone to get through the work. In 1912, I made some tracings of the Friern Watch/Ravensdale/Mayfield Avenues, taking great care with them and left them on a windowsill to dry overnight. When I arrived the next morning, the police were there – the house had been burnt during the night. They said it was the work of suffragettes who had come from London. The police said that, in Friern Avenue, where there were some tiny cottages, an old lady had had toothache and couldn't sleep. She was walking up and down all night and saw the unusual sight of three or four cars going into Friern Watch House and coming out again. When they left the place was on fire.

The site was also a popular place for film production. It was used by Kalem Films who brought actors and scenery along. I became an interested bystander and once earned a packet of cigarettes by helping in one of the scenes. Further along Finchley, by the Green Man, there were two very fine houses which stood back called Brownswells which, in the last century, had some waters with medicinal powers. They were often used by film producers.

When I was demobilized after World War I, I had an invitation to join the staff of Hampstead Garden Suburb which was being developed by three non-profit making companies, each of whom was developing various areas of the suburb. The work they did

for housing roused others to take notice, including the borough councils. I met Dame Henrietta Barnett many times and used to lunch with her quite frequently. She was a person who thought a great deal of herself and even more of her departed husband Canon Barnett. One day, I was organizing a lunch and one of the chief guests was a man from the Isle of Wight, Lt-Col. Hobart. He had a perpetual 'blink' and he was sitting on one side of Dame Henrietta and I was on the other. They kept up a conversation and things went very well but he couldn't stop blinking. After coffee had been served and it was time to go, the Colonel turned to Dame Henrietta with a wink and said, 'Shall we go for a walk round the boundaries, Henrietta?' She was shocked!

She was a great believer in health food and anyone who dined with her

Their Majesties King George V & Queen Mary. Leaving the "Haven of Rest," Hampstead Tenants Ltd (Hampstead Garden Suburb) on March 18th 1911.

A royal visit to Hampstead Garden Suburb in 1911.

The Hog Market in East Finchley was an area of poor housing. A bomb during the Second World War destroyed much of the property seen here.

was always extolled to use Bemax [a wheat germ product] and she often said to me 'Young man, you should be taking Bemax'. I said, 'What's wrong with me?' and she replied, 'Nothing wrong but look how different you would be if you took Bemax.' I used it for many years and it didn't seem to do me any harm.

Public Service

I was a member of the Congregational church at East Finchley who, like other churches, were awakening to the affects of poor housing. Worthy new houses were not being built in sufficient numbers. I was asked to serve on a committee which brought me into touch with slums. Later, I had an invitation to stand for the East Ward of Finchley Council which I did in 1923. Poor housing was generally accepted in the 1920s and there was no one to give expression to the problem. Finchley was an unknown, quiet sufferer of bad housing – places such as Market Place and Prospect Place in East Finchley, which were built around 1812 or 1820.

I was re-elected to the council and served from 1923 to 1933, by which time I became Chairman of the Urban District Council. My interest in housing spread all over the borough and I got to know places in North Finchley that were as bad as East Finchley. My work, and that of my contemporaries in local government, was taken very seriously – looking back on it perhaps too seriously. We enjoyed the work because we had the co-operation of the Chief Officers and enjoyed it because we had the unseen but ever-present eye of the public watching us. There was no party politics, which has undoubtedly ruined local government.

23

Finchley fire brigade outside its Hendon Lane station just after its horse-drawn appliance had been replaced by a motorized unit. The brigade comprised both full- and part-time firemen and was moved to a purpose-built station in Long Lane around 1930.

In one period I was on the Highways Committee, who were responsible for the fire brigade. We had a fire station in Hendon Lane, just by the parish church, with a horse-drawn engine. One evening, after a meeting of the committee, we thought we would give the fire brigade a test call. We went up to The Spaniards (at Hampstead) which was the end of our boundary and pulled the alarm and stood there with our watches. About ten minutes later, the horse-drawn engine arrived. Later on, the Fire Officer arrived by bicycle which was kept at The King of Prussia. We congratulated the brigade on their performance. We then made a mistake. At the next committee meeting we did the same again, this time in the Barnet area ... pulled the alarm. Nothing happened: nobody turned up. We went back to the fire station in Hendon Lane

and asked why they hadn't turned up. 'Well, we knew it was a false alarm, like last month', they replied.

On educational matters, I am very proud that, in the mid-Thirties, I had a lot to do with Our Lady of Lourdes School which had made an application through the Westminster Diocesan Council. Finchley turned it down. 'We're not going to have a Roman Catholic school in Finchley', they decided. I thought they had made a good case and eventually I broke down the opposition and they got their school, since when they have been very gracious towards me. Later, I went to Rome on behalf of the World Health Organization. I was doing a survey of housing progress in different European capitals which took me to Rome, among others. One morning in the hotel, I received a letter from the Vatican inviting me to an audience with the Pope that morning. I was received by him in his private study and we talked about education and Our Lady of Lourdes School and he thanked me for the help I had given. It was a great thrill.

One thing which I attach great importance to is the Brookside Walk. It starts at Falloden Way in the Garden Suburb, goes along the brook to Henly's Corner, crosses over and up to the borough boundary. Now, I was in Cologne for a conference between the wars and was taken by their Town Clerk and Burgomaster around the original town walls which had become a public walk with lovely gardens. I thought, why can't we turn our brook-side into a walk? I worked away at it and Finchley Council agreed to pursue it but when we got as far as Westbury Road where the gardens went right down to the brook, we were bunkered. Our only hope was to see if Hendon would acquire the piece of land on their side so that we had a cross-over. I discussed it with my opposite number in Hendon and he thought it a good idea so now we get to Westbury Road, cross over into Hendon and go right the way along to where Lullington Garth starts and then back eventually into Finchley. [Ed.: With the formation of the London Borough of Barnet in 1965, when Finchley and Hendon were amalgamated, such problems were easier to resolve and the borough today has a network of splendid walks within its boundaries.]

The high spot of my career was being made Mayor of Finchley in 1937/38 and 1958/59 and three periods as Chairman of the Urban Council before we became a borough. What stands out is the consciousness that, as Mayor of Finchley, at the wonderful banquet evening, you have been chosen by your fellow councillors. That's an inspiration and it's not something felt by all mayors up and down the country.

Alfred Pike
Recorded December 1980

The Ingleway Estate off Summers Lane, built in 1921, was a typical example of the local council's efforts to meet the demands for more and better housing.

CHAPTER 4
The Actor's Tale

Finchley Garden Village, c. 1910.

A strong community spirit existed in Finchley Garden Village. Morris dancing was one of the many activities enjoyed by the residents.

I was born in Stoke Newington in January 1902 and we moved to Dollis Road, Finchley, when I was three. My father, among other things, was a professional singer – solo bass at St Nicholas in the City and a member of the Westminster Cathedral choir. One day, out walking, he found some houses being built by the Dollis Brook and they said a Garden Village was starting and he put our name down for one of the houses. We moved in in 1908.

My father also sang in a male voice quartet who rehearsed in our house at least twice a week. One day, when I was about four, they sat me on the piano and I 'sang' a song. They passed a bowler hat around and collected 3s 9d – the first money I ever earned.

Stephen Jack is my professional name. My real name is Hutchinson and my father Charles Hutchinson advised me to use two of my Christian names if I insisted upon being an actor because he said he was constantly being confused with at least four other actors who had similar names. So I pushed the boat out in 1919 when I started.

I was at Finchley County School for six years. It was during an Easter holiday that one of the village people, Walter McEwan, already in the acting profession, asked if I had ever thought about becoming an actor. I had, in fact, appeared for three nights in the Theatre Royal, Kings Lynn, in a play called *Captain Drew on Leave* that my father was in. They had lost a young man from the company and I was already six foot tall and my voice had broken. It whetted my appetite for the stage. McEwan told me that he was acting with Fred Terry in *The Scarlet Pimpernel* and that Terry was looking for a tall young man to complete his company for the next tour.

I got the job and, fortunately for me, it was an all-costume play and I didn't have to provide any clothes. I couldn't have done because I only had the jacket and trousers I stood up in! I had just turned seventeen. Fred gave a magnificent performance as the Pimpernel even though he was around sixty, rather overweight, had gout very badly and sometimes couldn't even go on. As soon as he opened his mouth and started playing, I'm quite sure every one in the audience forgot about his age and size.

Later on, I went on tour with the Arts League Travelling Theatre, which was a marvellous experience. We were a small company of ten, with a driver, and we all sang, danced and acted. It was run by a woman called Eleanor Elder who had been a professional actress. She got together people who afterwards became very famous, such as the two Baddeley sisters, Angela and Hermione, Andrew Cruikshank and John Pertwee, and we went by road everywhere in a converted van which carried all our scenery and costumes, folding furniture and personal effects. We went all over the place, including one or two public schools. The purpose of the thing was to show local people how easy and cheap it was to put on their own entertainment in their own village hall or school. Generally, our bill consisted of two one-act plays and eight or nine short items such as folk songs and dances. I spent two years with them, touring England, Scotland and Wales. I started off at £3 per week, which was pocket money

Finchley County School around 1902.

because we were put up by local people and never knew whether we would be staying with a duke or a dustman. Therefore we had to be very good mixers and behave well. I look back on it with great affection.

I joined the Actors' Church Union: Lillian Bayliss was a member of the Council. I also served on the Council and when, in 1925, I came off a tour with a Somerset Maugham play, Lillian asked me take over from John Laurie who was going to Stratford. I played the ghost in *Hamlet* to Ernest Milton's Hamlet, a fine actor whose Hamlet has never been bettered or equalled. Then I played in a modern-dress *Hamlet* in the autumn of 1925 with the Birmingham Rep. It was the first time that Shakespeare had been done in modern dress.

I learned acting the hard way. I didn't do any formal dramatic training – very few people then went to drama school. It's a very good way to learn but would be impossible today because you have to be reasonably good before you have a hope of getting a part and then you're playing in competition with at least ten other people.

In 1936, I returned to London after playing at the Liverpool Playhouse for five years. I had some experience with radio broadcasting. In 1926 I played *Hassan* with Norman Shelley at 2LO, Savoy Hill, so I thought I would have a shot at the BBC. I liked radio but had not thought of it as a main line in my career. I went to Broadcasting House to see the man in charge of the Drama Booking Department, Bruce Belfridge,

and he asked me to read something. I told him I specialized in doing accents so he handed me a piece to do. About a fortnight later, I got my first job in BBC Radio. I asked the producer, a very friendly man, what gave them the idea of asking me to do this part. He said, 'Well, Bruce Belfridge said you can do any bloody accent under the sun.' So I was now on track and after that I played lots of parts which required an Irish or Norfolk accent or something like that. I did about two different transmissions a week and sometimes two a day if there was a schools programme or *Children's Hour*. I played every part in *Toytown* (except Larry the Lamb) and Owl or Rabbit in *Winnie the Pooh*. It was a marvellous job – very, very enjoyable and I can't remember anything I've been involved in that has given me greater happiness than working in *Children's Hour*.

Stephen Jack
Recorded November 1984

CHAPTER 5

The Law Officer's Tale

The regimental band of the Middlesex Regiment practising at Inglis Barracks, Mill Hill, *c.* 1924.

Friern Barnet library in 1924. It was one of the buildings used by the Juvenile Employment Bureau in which school-leavers were interviewed to place them in suitable jobs.

I was born in Latymer Grove, Hammersmith in 1883. When I was a boy at school I did a paper round early in the morning. On one or two mornings it made me late for school and I got a damn good caning for it. One day, I got a caning on both hands and round my legs by the head teacher and I took the cane from him and told him not to hit me again. He took me up to his little room and said he would deal with me later. On the floor was a big pile of slates [used for writing]. He came into the room and said 'Pick up a handful of those slates and hold them over your head.' I refused. I think corporal punishment made us worse.

One day, in 1900, when I was coming home from visiting an old aunt who was fond of me, I saw an army recruiting sergeant in Hammersmith Broadway who asked me if I had a match. I gave him one and he put his fingers up to his ear and took out a dirty little cigarette end. I told him that it was not a very nice thing for a sergeant in the Queen's uniform to smoke and gave him a packet of cigarettes. He got talking about the army and asked me if I liked it. I said 'yes' but was not old enough – I was just under seventeen. He said he would put that right and I filled in the papers to join the Middlesex Regiment and he said to meet him at the courthouse at ten o'clock the following morning. I met him at the court and was handed over. He gave me a railway ticket to go and report in to Dover Castle and if I didn't go I would be a deserter. My parents were upset!

I got to Dover Castle in the evening and went into a large barrack room with about forty beds in it. I didn't like to get undressed that night in front of the men in the barrack room. I said 'turn the lights out and I'll get into bed.' In those days, if there were no NCOs on the spot, an old soldier used to take charge. We used to have a recreation room where you could get a cup of coffee, which was nearly a mile from the barrack square. One morning (I'd been in the army about a week) an old soldier told me to go and buy him a packet of Woodbines. I refused, got put on a 'fizzer' (a charge) and got seven days' CB (confined to barracks). You then did all the dirty jobs in the barracks and cleaned and whitewashed the cells. While I was doing this, a sergeant came in and got a splash of whitewash on his clothes. I got another seven days' CB! After that, I did everything possible to be a good boy in the army.

I went to Hounslow in 1903 and stayed there and places such as Mill Hill until I was chucked out in 1920. I left with the rank of Regimental Sergeant Major. I thought, 'I need a suit of decent clothes to get a decent job', so I went to

A typical church school in the borough: St James's School, Friern Barnet Lane, in around 1906.

Milk delivery boys were often illegally employed and, as such, were a target for the Law Officer.

the Strand and got a couple of made-to-measure suits for £3 each. I saw an announcement in the *Daily Telegraph* that Law Officers were wanted to look after school departments – that sort of thing – and went to the Guildhall, Westminster, for an interview. They appointed me and asked me where I lived. In those days, Southgate Education covered Southgate, Friern Barnet, Potters Bar, High Barnet and outlying districts where people lived in one area and went to school in another.

One day, the Ministry of Labour decided that they would have Juvenile Employment Bureaux opened up all over the country. Every borough would have one and I was appointed to be trained. The job was to interview all children leaving school and put them into suitable employment. When we started, my boss, Mr Smales, and the Local Education Officer said we would have to get a committee together and I got together a panel of about fourteen industrialists, schoolmasters and local people. We were based at Bowes Road School and I had other offices at Potters Bar and in the Friern Barnet library. I built up committees in each district and we had about 300-400 children apply every year. When the council finally handed over the job, they invited me to a dinner at which they showed that I had placed 22,000 boys and girls into jobs.

Part of my job as a Law Officer was to catch truants from local schools. You can always tell a boy playing 'hookey'. He'd look at you out of the corner of his eye and say something like 'I don't feel well today and don't like to go to school.' I can tell you that there are many prominent people today who played 'hookey'! The law was that you had to see the child back to school. It used to be a curse. Young children would be out delivering milk with a milkman at five o'clock in the morning. Needless to say, I used to be out at five o'clock too on my motorbike, walk round a corner and if I saw a boy out before seven o'clock, I would ask him what he was doing and who he worked for. It might be, say, a local dairy and I would tell them they were breaking the law. They would say 'we don't employ them' but they were responsible and I would tell them that if there was any more, I'd be around after them. If they persisted, I would take the employer to the County Council Committee who would decide if they would take them to court. When I started in 1920, there were plenty of cases. Girls would be out at 6 a.m. scrubbing doorsteps. A child needed a special certificate to work before 7 a.m.

Arthur C. Froude
Recorded January 1979

CHAPTER 6

North Finchley Remembered

St John's Cottages (right) with The Triumph pub in the background, 1999.

Woodhouse Lane (now Woodhouse Road) as it looked in the early years of the twentieth century.

I was born on Boxing Day 1896 in Old Street. We moved to Finchley when I was two and a half years old because my father bought two businesses in Summers Lane next to the Triumph pub. One was a confectioner's and the other a small grocer's shop which the Co-op was after but never got. We lived above the grocer's shop in No. 4 St John's Cottages, Summers Lane, (listen carefully!) New Southgate; it became North Finchley later. When we first came, the cottage was lit by oil lamps and then by gas. My father was the first to have electricity in the area, about 1908. It cost £10 to put on – we bought the cable in. The Triumph got it for nothing.

The cottage had two bedrooms, a parlour, a kitchen, a coal cellar under the shop and a stable outside for the horses and trap. They were driven by 'Weasel' Turner who took people to

Southgate station for trains to Kings Cross. Horse buses went as far as the Swan & Pyramids when they changed horses and went back to town along Regents Park Road. I believe another branch went to Highgate.

As a youngster, I went to Albert Street School and was there for nine years. I walked to school up Woodhouse Lane, as it was then called, where the trees reached each other across the lane. Woodhouse belonged to Mr Wright-Ingle. I remember a house called Kimberley near the corner of Grove Road which had a parrot in the porch which said regular at five minutes to nine, 'Come on you children, it's five to nine.' I remember my first months at school (1901) when I was five because they started dishing up food instead of going home. For a penny you got a bowl of soup and a piece of bread which I didn't like so I went home. The teachers

36

I remember are Mr Preston, I was in his class, and Miss Lee, who came by bike from Wood Green.

We had a carpenter's shop in the playground to teach the boys woodwork and other boys came from Whetstone and Stanhope Road School. When King Edward [VII] was crowned we were given a coronation mug and marched to Grove Road, which was then all fields, and had a sing-song and tea. I was a good scholar until I was eleven years old when I got rheumatic fever. I was so light-headed that I find it difficult to remember. I was wrapped in cotton wool to make you sweat. I was in Finchley Memorial Hospital in 1906 although the hospital opened officially in 1908. There were about seven patients in there.

Before I left school, I worked for pocket money at Miss Schelt's nursery in Ballards Lane. The manager was Mr Kemp who was head fireman at the fire station in Hendon Lane. They grew all sorts including flowers. When the flowers were blooming, I had the job at weekends, before the flowers went to Convent Garden Market by horse and cart, of putting gum in the centre of the bloom so that the petals wouldn't fall off. They left at 2 a.m.

I remember the trams coming through. About 1903 they laid rails and put down the blocks. The first Tally Ho! to New Southgate trams turned back at the railway bridge at New Southgate because the bridge couldn't stand the weight. You walked over the bridge and caught another tram there to Wood Green! For one penny you could ride from Totteridge Lane, change at

Construction of Finchley Cottage Hospital was first considered as part of Queen Victoria's Diamond Jubilee in 1897, but it was not opened until 1908.

Tally Ho! corner with its trams, *c.* 1908.

Tally Ho! and go on to the Orange Tree in Friern Barnet.

Courting

We used to pick up girls in those days in what was called 'Monkey's Parade' which stretched from today's Sainsburys [Ravensdale Avenue] to Woodhouse Lane. The servant girls from the big houses had Wednesday nights off. I did my courting on the racecourse. It was where Woodberry Way and the tram depot [recently demolished] now stands. The rails and posts were still there.

Entertainment

My father used to hire for £5, once a year, the Leg of Mutton pond in Upway, Summers Lane. It was for ice skating and he had a stall there to sell hot drinks, hot potatoes and so on.

When I was a boy, Finchley Carnival used to be a carnival! Up to the First World War it used to start by Oakleigh Road and go through Whetstone, up Ballards Lane into East End Road, turn left at the Bald Faced Stag and finish at Tally Ho! There were floats, bands and hundreds watched it. Mr Yates, the manager of Marshall's, led the carnival on horse. They had a fête and fair every year to raise funds where Finchley Memorial Hospital now stands.

The first cinema I went to was where Advance Laundries is today [Ed.: No longer! It was opposite Ravensdale Avenue]. It was in a big tent and there were bench seats with a stage and screen at one end. At the very first show, we went under the side of the tent and we kids were so frightened because it was a train that came towards us – we all ran out and got a clip round the ear from the attendant. I believe the first purpose-built cinema was the New Hall which became so busy that they called it the Grand Hall: I saw Pearl White there.

They opened another picture palace in Stanhope Road and my friend Harold Littlewood used to play a wind-up gramophone.

Avenue House

You are talking to the fellow now who, when the Council took over Avenue House around 1929, had the rotten job of finding out which sewers were going into the manhole. I put on overalls and went down a 35ft ladder into a kind of well at the back of the house. There were about five different inlets coming into the wall. When I was drying myself around the fire, and

Finchley Carnival in 1907. The carnival was extremely popular and an important fund-raiser for Finchley Memorial Hospital.

had lit up a fag, the manager, Mr Bayliss, came in and said 'Put that cigarette out. What are you doing down there?' I said 'I'm drying myself out', and threw the job in! After doing all that, that's how they treated you in those days.

Joe Howe
Recorded May 1981

New Hall, North Finchley,
122 HIGH STREET,
Doors open 5.45.   Commence at 6.

HIGH-CLASS
Motion Picture Hall,
Showing a continuous performance of all up-to-date subjects and Foreign Scenes including Industries, History, Drama Comic, etc., etc., from 6 p.m.

Programme changed Twice Weekly.
TUESDAY & FRIDAY.

Prices 3d. & 6d.   Children 2d. & 3d

Matinee on Saturday at 2 and Thursday at 3 o'clock.

Children under 14 admitted for 1d. and 2d. on Saturday afternoon.

A local newspaper advertisement for the New Hall cinema, 1910.

Avenue House was built in 1858. It was bought by H.C. Stephens (of Stephens' Ink fame) around 1878 and, upon his death, was left to the people of Finchley.

CHAPTER 7

The Tweeny's Tale

Mr Mitchell's class in Bell Lane School, c. 1916.

Parson Street, Hendon, c. 1900.

I was born on 9 October 1904 and we came to Hendon in 1909. I went to Bell Lane School but I was not happy there – they had so many favourites among the better-off families who were treated better than working-class children.

I left school at fourteen to go into service. It was easy to get a job in service and my first was at Derby House in Parson Street (opposite The Downage) as an in-between maid. The owners of the house were Mr and Mrs Kilburn and I heard about the job from Olivers' the butcher in Church End. Mrs Kilburn interviewed me and offered me 7s 6d per week; paid monthly and living in. I only ever saw the lady of the house on pay day and I never saw the master all the time I worked there.

There were three servants: the house parlour-maid, the cook and myself. They also had a gardener and a huge kitchen garden where they grew all their own vegetables, soft fruit and flowers. There were two bedrooms for the servants and I shared with the parlour-maid who, incidentally, was the cook's sister. We had a bed each but I shared a chest-of-drawers and we had a jug and basin for washing. On the landing was a bathroom with a bath encased in mahogany and when there was any hot water we occasionally had a bath. The family had its own bathroom.

I got up at 6 a.m. and my first job was to clean the kitchen range (black-lead and so on) and light the fire. The range had a steel fender which was cleaned with a piece of leather with chains in it. There was no emery paper and it was hard work. I then made tea and took it to the cook. Breakfast finished about 8 a.m. and we would then go upstairs and sweep the bedroom and clean the windows – every day! One unusual thing I remember about the house was that it had a dumb-waiter from the basement kitchen to the dining room. We also cleaned the drawing room – a huge lounge with a parquet floor – and we then had our midday meal which, for us, was the main meal of the day. After the meal, I helped prepare the vegetables for the family's meal and wash up after our own. The family had dinner at 7 p.m.

We had a huge semi-basement kitchen and scullery, a large

A typical cast-iron kitchen range and fender, both of which required regular cleaning.

Dr Andrews in his pony and trap in Holders Hill, Hendon.

larder with a blue slate shelf where meat was kept under the wire gauze covers and a shallow porcelain sink. The house had high railings at the front with two or three marble steps leading up to a beautiful Victorian front door. I had to clean those steps every morning as well as do all the washing up and washing the kitchen.

The family did a lot of entertaining. He was the Kilburn of Kilburn & Shaw, the motor people, although they didn't have a car. They entertained every weekend when they rolled up the carpet and danced to one of those gramophones with a large horn. I stayed about twelve months because I didn't like living in.

We were sometimes short of money at home and my mother had to go without so we children could be fed. There was a local Board of Guardians, (the man's name was Mr Bone) and my mother went to him. He said 'I will lend you 2s 6d but you have got to bring it back to me'. My mother used to go out on Monday washing and ironing from nine in the morning until nine o'clock at night and all she earned was one half-crown! That was just before the 1914-18 war.

From ten years of age I worked every Saturday morning scrubbing steps for sixpence but you could buy a loaf of bread and a pound of sugar for that. We lived in Fuller Street. There was one scullery and one lavatory between two houses. They were good neighbours.

The poor helped the poor. When we were ill, Dr Andrews, who lived on the corner of Babington Road, would call. He was a good man. A woman came round every week and we paid her fourpence for the doctor's service. He made up the medicine in his own surgery – there were no chemist's shops then.

My most abiding childhood memory perhaps won't appeal to many people. I was passionately fond of dolls and we had a little toy shop which I used to pass on my way to school. You could buy china-headed dolls which cost 1s 6d and 2s 6d, which was a lot of money. Now I have a collection of them. Once things settled down after the First World War, goods in the shops were very reasonable in price. When I was nineteen years old, for example, I got a beautiful costume from Selfridge's for 19s 11d. They also sold delicious ice-cream sundaes for 9d – a huge cone-shaped glass with fruit – and a lovely dinner cost 1s 6d.

Things did get better. More modern inventions came in. For example, in a Sydney Grove house at which I worked, they had a vacuum cleaner but it was a wooden affair with a handle and a long pipe and I used to have to pull the handle backwards and forwards to get the suction. Gas stoves came in but they still had to be black-leaded and we even had an electric iron which was a big step forward. Celluloid cuffs and collars were another good idea.

Florence Hanson
Recorded January 1981

CHAPTER 8

The Doctor's Tale

Hendon Cottage Hospital was opened in 1913 and extended in 1925 and 1933 to meet a growing demand. It closed in 1987 and was demolished in the early 1990s.

Mill Hill School in the 1920s.

I was born on 2 February 1891 in the small North Lincolnshire town of Barton-upon-Humber. My grandfather and father were in practice there before me. My grandfather started in 1836 before the introduction of anaesthetics and a long time before the introduction of antiseptic surgery. There were great limitations in those days: abdominal surgery, for example, was almost impossible. The idea was to get an operation over as quickly as possible to shorten the time of the patient's suffering. Amputations were done at an incredible speed.

My father was in practice from about 1875 until 1920. Up to 1909, he had a horse and trap and, before that, rode a horse. There were no telephones then. If you wanted the doctor you had to call upon him. When I was a boy, in 1900, we had the first telephone installed in Barton-upon-Humber.

I decided to go into medicine from very early days. I was able to watch my father who was a first-class general practitioner and I couldn't think of any better occupation. When I went to a small school in Stoke Newington with my two brothers, we all took matriculation and went to London Hospital. There were some great people there like Sir Robert Hutchison* – one of the greatest teachers of medicine that I ever knew. He was elected President of the Royal College of Physicians, London. I qualified in 1915, the first full year of the war, went into the

*Note: Hanging on the doctor's wall was a framed copy of the so-called Hutchison Litany to which he attached both importance and affection. It says:
'From inability to leave well alone,
For too much zeal for the new and from contempt for what is old,
From putting knowledge before wisdom, science before art and cleverness before common sense.
From treating patients as cases, and
From making the cure of the disease more grievous than the endurance of the same.
Good Lord deliver us'.

Royal Army Medical Corps and spent the rest of the war in Greece.

I came to Mill Hill in 1921. My brother and I joined an elderly practitioner in partnership with him in Hammers Lane. My brother, who had come the year before, lived in Langley Park. When old Dr Martin died, after a couple of years, we got another partner who was with us for most of the time we were in practice. We had a first-class surgeon who operated, sometimes in emergencies, but generally once a week on Friday and we used to go and assist him and sometimes give the anaesthetic. The doctors in the Mill Hill and Hendon area kept in close contact with each other because we all met at the Cottage Hospital.

The National Insurance Act had come in by 1911 and most of the men came under that and were not charged at all – the panel it was called. Wives and families did not come in until 1948. I think, although I can't remember. We charged them 3s 6d a visit. The area was very mixed indeed in terms of social classes. We were medical officers at Mill Hill School; there were not a great many wealthy people; large numbers of middle-class people and poorer people from the Mill Hill East area. In fact, the more varied a practice is, the better it is from the medical point of view and the more interesting. It is a great mistake to imagine that a practice with wealthy people is the best. It is not.

In the 1920s, there were a number of infectious diseases which in my grandfather's day were fatal. Diphtheria, for example, was common then but has been virtually wiped out with immunization. For example, I remember my father saying that, in our small Lincolnshire town during an outbreak of diphtheria, there was a vicar who had eight children. Six weeks later, he had only four. Pneumonia was a great killer before antibiotics. When I started medicine, the general death rate from pneumonia in England and Wales was 20 per cent. Today, it is below 1 per cent. There was malnutrition in the area and rickets was quite common. You rarely see it these days.

The two greatest changes in my times were the introduction of antibiotics, particularly penicillin, which has saved an enormous number of lives; the other is the frightful results of cigarette smoking. Lung cancer, in the early days, was so rare that you just didn't see it at all. The total deaths from it in England and Wales in 1910 was 390. During the course of fifty years it is now 58,000 per annum. It can only be dealt with by preventing people from smoking – particularly cigarettes.

One of the great dangers in medicine today is for a doctor to rely too much on X-rays and laboratory reports. If you follow them too closely, you can sometimes go completely wrong. There is no substitute for taking a careful history, listening to what the patient had to say and a reasonable examination of the patient. Short cuts can mislead. If people rely upon computers to make a diagnosis not only will they frequently be completely wrong but their brains will atrophy!

A.H.M.
Recorded April 1979

CHAPTER 9

The Tram Driver's Tale

The Kingsway in North Finchley was laid out in 1933. Several tram routes merged at this point, which was adjacent to the tram depot in Woodberry Grove.

125" FINCHLEY'S FIRST ELECTRIC TRAMCAR

Finchley's first electric tramcar shows how exposed the driver was to the elements. Later designs, with such refinements as a windscreen, improved matters. The inside of the tram was luxurious by comparison!

Laying tram rails in the High Road, North Finchley, c. 1902. The tramway required the cutting down of many of the fine trees which lined the road – an act which caused considerable anger among local residents.

I was born on 12 June 1908 at Wood Green. My father was a professional musician. He had been a band boy in the Royal Navy but was invalided out and died of TB when he was thirty-five – three months before I was born.

About 1930, our family doctor advised me, after my sister had died of TB, to get a job on the outside, working in the fresh air. So I applied for the trams. It was never advertised and the only time people were taken on was May to September when the regular men had their holidays. The work was therefore seasonal and you could only get on permanent staff by natural wastage. I applied to the Manor House offices in Seven Sisters Road which was the Metropolitan Electric Tramway's area office. We were stuck in a room all day long, starting at 9 a.m. and were not interviewed until 3 p.m. when the first man went in.

I was accepted and did my training at the Acton Broadway Depot of London United Tramway, a sister company of MET. You started as a temporary conductor to 'learn the route' and there was no difference in pay between a conductor and a driver (or motorman as he is more properly called). At the Public Carriage Office in Lambeth Road you got your badge (numbered in my case 20070) and a big licence, about 2ft by 1ft, which folded into a case which you carried with you at all time.

At the time of which I speak, there was the 21 tram which ran from North Finchley to Holborn via Wood Green and Finsbury Park. North Finchley was my depot and, later, as a driver, I was almost entirely on the 21s and 19s which ran from Barnet to Euston. We worked a 96-hour fortnight – which is not the same as a 48-hour week! One week was 'cushy'. On the 21s, for example, you would do three journeys (i.e. there and back) to Holborn which was 6 hours and a 36-hour week. On the next week you worked 60 hours – the first tram went out about 4 a.m. The last tram, on the 19s, went into the depot at 1.30 a.m.; the service was every 6 to 8 minutes.

After two years of conducting I went on a three-week course to learn driving. At Acton, they had a mock-up of a tram and the instructor showed us the different parts of the tram – the trolley, the cow-catcher, the dog-gate and so on. We were properly trained: he would send us out of the room and make 'faults' which we had to find. For example, he would put a piece of paper between the wheel in the trolley-head so that it would not make contact with the wire.

After leaving the school, you went with another motorman and this was your real training for another two or three weeks, learning a number of routes. The art of good tram driving was not to build up speed too fast and not to stop with too much force.

The main cause of friction between the conductor and driver was rough driving and running late, which

The tram depot in Woodberry Grove was demolished in 1998.

resulting in picking up too many passengers. Another thing was 'over-riding' where a passenger would try to go beyond the fare stage. So prevalent was this that many conductors would punch a ticket on the line to avoid being booked and claim, if an inspector came aboard, that the tram had jerked as he was punching the ticket.

We were issued with good Melton clothes – better than the police. Thick Melton trousers, a three-quarter length jacket and overcoat plus oilskins. I have stood on the open trams and it was as if you had nothing on at all! They were very cold. I wore gauntlets all the year round although they weren't issued and I always bought my own hat although they were issued. When I started in 1930, the wage was about £3 per week. My wife was a good manager and I was able to send my sons to grammar school. Holidays were strange. You got ten days' paid holiday but you had to be on three years before you qualified. It seemed as if the holidays were drawn out of a hat with the people who did the drawing, the Union officials, invariably seeming to get Junes and Julys. For several years I got Septembers and Octobers. I didn't feel the unions were effective. They didn't want to offend the guv'nors and take positive action. I found them very ineffective.

Around 1933, I was driving an open 62 tram at Wembley church, which is in the middle of an S-bend. I was coming down the hill when coming up, on the wrong side, was a huge steam traction engine with leading wheels about 10ft in diameter. We met on my side of the road with the biggest crash you've ever heard. The boiler burst, steam came out and his axle broke. Here was I standing on an open tram trying to operate toe brakes. A large piece of glass came down from the tram's upper saloon window like a guillotine blade and onto my gloved wrist. Fortunately, it just cut the glove and not my wrist. The traction engine was pulled on to the side of the road and remained there until it was red rust. I suppose they couldn't get spare parts for it. I had to take the tram back to the Finchley depot myself and it was back in service in a fortnight. So those old trams were well built.

I remember during a spell of conducting in 1936 being handed an Edward VIII threepenny piece which I paid in at night. It's quoted today as being worth £3,000!

Tom Relph
Recorded January 1981

CHAPTER 10
Childhood Memories of Hendon

Horse-drawn cabs plied for trade outside the Hendon LMS station in Station Road. Many of the new houses being built were some distance from the station and cabs would drive along the residential roads at breakfast time to see if their services were required.

Brent Street, c. 1905. This was one of the main shopping centres in the area. Nearby Bell Lane was a terminus for buses and cabs and boasted a public lavatory located beneath ground level.

I was born in Paddington in 1895. It was a depressed area then but fashionable today. We came to Hendon when I was seven, that is 1902, and we lived in Sunningfields Crescent. To get there, my younger brother and I came to the Hendon Midland Station (LMS) and from there in a four-wheel cab. As we turned the bend in the Crescent, I had my first view of the country – sheep were grazing opposite our house. The Council had the common sense in the 1920s to buy the land – it is now Sunnyhill Park.

My father was a chartered accountant and we were just about comfortably off. We had a maid a good deal of the time and I'm ashamed to think we paid her badly but they all were in those days. She was formerly a Dr Barnardo's child. One girl I remember was a local one. When she took us out occasionally in the afternoon we went to this girl's house and were bribed with sweets to say nothing. My mother

thought we were walking and getting the good air.

When I was seven, I went to Ravenshurst School which was opposite where the library stands today. The building is now demolished. It was a private school run by the Misses Eliza and Emily Grouse. Miss Eliza was a priceless old dear who coped with the domestic side of the school – they had a few boarders. Miss Emily dealt with the educational side. They had a music teacher, which meant that lots of children had private music lessons and singing.

The age range was five to seven and then up to sixteen when you took an exam. There were about seventy children in the school and the education was very strange. I didn't do much maths. Miss Emily was frightfully keen on literature – she knew an awful lot about the subject and we read out loud Shakespeare plays at much too young an age. We had an excellent visiting gym mistress and I loved gym.

Miss Emily was very kind and interesting. I remember two occasions I had to be a boarder because of illness in our family and always in the evenings we used to go to Miss Emmie's sitting room and sit round an open fire while she read or told stories – which was unusual for those days. She commanded respect and never had to hit anyone with a stick. We had a so-called 'rough book' in which we wrote anything we liked but you never had time to write properly when taking notes. That's why my writing is so appalling today.

Every summer we did a play for the parents. Once we did *A Midsummer Night's Dream* and I played one of the fairies. I was a boarder at the time and my mother made me a lovely dress and wings for the fairy part. When we came teetering through the orchard (it was an open air performance) my mother was horrified to see that her dear little fairy had her knickers a long way below her dress and were not too clean at that. Poor mother had to rush from her seat in the interval and tell the staff to put a clean pair of knickers on her daughter.

When they (the Grouses) retired, having made very little money on the school, they lived in Heriot Road, Hendon. Little Em during the winter months used to do a series of lectures on some poet or writer and nearly all the old parents used to come and support her and pay a shilling a time. In the end, the old girls from the school formed a fund which helped them for some years.

The shops in Hendon before the First World War were quite good, useful and all that was needed at the time. There

Sunningfields Road, leading into Sunningfields Crescent as it looked in the early 1920s. Some of the trees still survive but, at most times, today's street is lined on both sides with motor cars.

The Burroughs Pond, Hendon, *c.* 1900. The low white buildings on the right were replaced by the Quadrant Close block of flats in 1934 and little remains of the pond itself.

was an excellent greengrocer, for example, who used to bring his goods around two or three times a week in an open basket. You would order from the open basket and it would be delivered later by a boy. Personal service was important.

There was little public transport. You used your own two feet. My father preferred walking to the Midland station, about 1½ miles, rather than take a cab. But there were one or two cabs who, on a wet day, used to drive around Sunningfields Crescent and look in the windows as we were having breakfast and wave their whips to see if we would like them to pick us up. There was an old man living up the road from us who had a tricycle. He used to ride to the station every morning taking with him his crook-stick. In the evening, he waited until someone was going up the hill in a four-wheeler and would hook his stick on the back axle and get taken up the hill. He was called 'Old Snuffy' from his habit of twitching his nose.

It was a local bus, I believe, which used to go two or three times a week from Bell Lane through Church Road and Station Road to the Midland station to meet the trains. But the driver loved his bottle of drink! If he had been in The Bell too long, he had to make up time to the station so did a short cut through Brampton Grove which meant that those waiting in Church Road never saw the bus. They had been bypassed. My mother told the tale of when she was coming back on the evening bus. The horses going up the hill at Station Road would go through the very nice horse pond at The Burroughs to sup the water. If the man had had too many in the pub he used to fall asleep and, if you were in a hurry to get home, you took off your shoes, lifted up your skirts, paddled across the shallow pond and walked home! It happened to her more than once.

Dorothy Egerton
Recorded December 1979

CHAPTER 11
A Wartime Tale:
The Women's Voluntary Service

The so-called Anderson shelter supplied during the early part of the Second World War was cold and damp but provided good protection against almost anything other than a direct hit.

Rescue workers and others were supplied with refreshments by the WVS. This bombed site in Hampstead Garden Suburb was one of a number in the area visited by the King and Queen.

Just before war broke out (September 1939), I was living in Bramber Road with my husband and two children aged seven and five. We had been on holiday in Broadstairs on the actual announcement of war and I remember returning to London by train and seeing barrage balloons all the way on the journey home.

Following government advice, we made our home as secure as possible. We shored up our dining room with great planks of wood against air raids. Every street was organized. I was asked by the Chairman of Bramber Road to become Secretary, which I accepted, and this was the beginning of my voluntary work. Two of the early tasks I remember were to get people to clear their attics of lumber (it was a fire risk)

and collecting all metal fences and gates down the road, plus aluminium pots and pans, and throwing them over the gates of the Town Hall.

I joined the Women's Voluntary Service (WVS) in February 1941. My first introduction was a 'sewing party' in Strathroy, a large house in Friern Barnet Lane which was the HQ of the ARP [Air-Raid Precautions] with a few rooms for WVS use. I was asked if I would take on the Emergency Feeding Unit for Friern Barnet and I agreed, taking my instructions from a Mr Morris who was in the Control Centre in the Town Hall.

The function of the unit was, when a bomb fell, to feed the people affected by the incident. To do this, we

Friern Barnet's
DIG FOR VICTORY WEEK
July 5th to 10th in Friary Park

A WEEK OF MANY EVENTS—BUT MAKE A SPECIAL NOTE OF THESE.

GRAND CONCERT and OPENING CEREMONY
At British Restaurant, Saturday July 3rd. Tickets 3/6 and 2/6 from 32, Glenthorne Road, N.11.   Enterprise 3120.

Opening Ceremony by CMDR. CAMPBELL
B.B.C. Brains Trust.

PRODUCE SHOW
On Friday & Saturday, July 9th & 10th in Friary Park

Opening by CYRIL FLETCHER and BETTY ASTELL

Prize Giving by MABEL CONSTANDUROS
Have you sent your entry form in yet ?

BRAINS TRUST
On Saturday, July 10th at 3 p.m. Friary Park Question Master FREDDIE GRISEWOOD, B.B.C.

OPENING OF THE EXHIBITION ON MONDAY JULY 5th at 2.30 p.m. by **RICHARD GOOLDEN** ("Mr. Penny")

TALKS BY **PERCY IZZARD** (Daily Mail) and other experts.

Poultry and Rabbit Show; Film Shows; Private Gardens Competition; Pigs and Bees Exhibition; Lectures; Talks and Demonstrations; Cookery Competition; Horticultural Exhibitions; Poultry Houses; Garden Frames; Childrens's Posters; Competitions for everyone.

200 Cash Prizes and Several Cups to be won.

This 'Dig for Victory Week' in June 1943 was designed to discourage people from going away for their holidays by offering, at local venues, attractive entertainment by well-known personalities.

had a number of feeding centres located in various parts of the area: Friary House, Oakleigh Road School, St Peter's School and Holly Park School come to mind. The centres housed stocks of tinned food and were staffed by a WVS team working on a rota basis – the idea being that the team nearest the incident would be called out. To do the job of cooking, we were supported by a Mobile Emergency Feeding Unit (MEFU) whose equipment was housed in the Advance Laundry in the High Road, Finchley. The unit comprised sheets of corrugated iron that made up into a kind of portable shed which could be quickly erected and a number of mobile wood-fired boilers on which the cooking was done.

An important part of our work was looking after the Repair Parties' canteens. When a bomb dropped, lots of men from the council and private builders were called to the site to undertake repairs. They needed light refreshments such as tea, coffee, rolls and cakes and, to do this, our canteen was set up near the incident, usually in a nearby damaged building which might have to be made safe for us to work in. For example, one of the worst incidents of the war was the flying bomb (V1) which fell in Russell Gardens just off Oakleigh Road killing young twins and doing widespread damage. We bought supplies of tea and so on from local traders. We made a 'good cup of tea' and I remember even today that one pint of milk was used for twenty-five cups.

National Savings Weeks, such as this 1943 'Wings for Victory' campaign advertised in a local shop, were just one of the numerous tasks undertaken by the WVS.

Waste food scraps, placed in dustbins at the end of the road, were collected by the WVS for turning into pig food.

Park, we carried a large tea urn around on one those 'stop me and buy one' Wall's ice cream tricycles.

National Savings weeks were another activity. These had titles such as 'Wings for Victory' and each area had a savings target. If you reached your target you were given a flag to fly. Artists such as Cyril Fletcher and Betty Astell gave concerts in support of the activity.

A more unusual service during wartime was the collection of food scraps for pig food. A number of dustbins were located in various streets into which local residents put their scraps and there were collected regularly by us for conversion into 'cakes' for local pigs. A Section Leader of the WVS was also responsible for running the so-called British Restaurants which would supply a good-quality lunch for around sixpence. One of the restaurants was in the Church Hall in Friern Barnet Lane and I worked every Sunday in it to provide, among others, a meal for the firemen over the road.

We also played a big part in the Holidays at Home scheme which was designed to encourage people to take their holidays locally rather than going away and using valuable transport and resources. To make it attractive, all sorts of events and entertainments were arranged in local parks. WVS provided the refreshments. Some of the famous people I remember who visited Friary Park at the time were Freddie Grisewood and Commander Campbell of the Brains Trust and the singers Ann Zeigler and Webster Booth who lived in Torrington Park and gave concerts in the Church Hall in Friern Barnet Lane. In Bethune

My voluntary work was seven days a week. The canteen opened at 9.30 a.m. and closed about 4 p.m. I made many friends at work and felt that I was making a real contribution to the war effort. There was a wonderful spirit among the people I worked with and the WVS never let anyone down, even elderly ladies such as Mrs Goddard and Miss Anderson worked very hard for the cause. The war brought people together and you made lots of friends.

Olive Dyke
Recorded February 1981

CHAPTER 12

The Funerary Mason's Tale

Kelly's Memorial Works in Holders Hill Road just before its closure in 1986.

David Moffatt, letter carver, in 1986.

I was born on 10 May 1905 at Crayford, Kent. My father, a local councillor in Crayford, was a millwright and in 1907 came to Finchley to work on Captain Scott's motor sledges with caterpillar tracks which were taken to the South Pole. They were built at Pope's Garage in Ballards Lane and we lived in Brownlow Road. My earliest memory is of my sister holding me over the bridge in Lover's Lane when a steam train passed under. I was terrified of trains for years.

I went to school in Squires Lane whose headmaster was Mr Mellor. During World War I, I was in the 7th Finchley Boy Scouts. The Group Scout Master was Mr Ackers. On one occasion, at a troop meeting, the lights went out and they said enemy raiders were coming over and to get home as soon as possible. I saw the German aeroplanes. During the day, the air-raid warning was given by a policeman on a bike with a notice on his back saying 'Take Cover'. Later on, they fired maroons from the Ballards Lane police station which exploded in the air. The all clear was sounded by Boy Scouts going round in a car blowing two notes on their bugles.

I left school at fourteen and got a job at Kelly's the funerary masons in Marylebone Road. My older brother worked there as a letter carver: he was self-taught. The firm had five branches and was owned by the Cramb family who, I heard from a member of the family, were emigrating to Australia but when they got to London, one of the children was taken ill with scarlet fever and had to go to hospital. So the parents stayed. The child was some weeks in hospital and Cramb went to work for Mr Kelly, a mason in Maida Vale. He became the manager when Mr Kelly died, scrubbed going to Australia and eventually became owner. They became one of the biggest funerary masons in London.

I was not officially apprenticed – it was a gentleman's agreement for five years. I got 10s a week for the first year and £1 the next until eventually I got about 50s. In the first year you were allowed to drill letters and fill them with lead but the skilled part (i.e. letter carving) you would not be trusted with. When you cut a letter in marble you can hardly see the edge of the letter so you put a red-ochre or red chalk on the stone and the white shows through. In polished granite, which is shiny and hard, you can't mark it. You can use a chinagraph pencil but usually you give it a coat of emulsion paint and then mark out the inscription. You then prime the cut letter and apply gold leaf.

There have been plenty of disasters! I had an inscription in Kingsbury church. The sexton, whose name was Noble, showed me the gravestone to be lettered for a Mr Chad. 'Are you sure that's the stone?' He said 'I ought to be. I dug the grave.' I put the inscription on it – it was the wrong one! It had to be chiselled off and rubbed down. You make spelling mistakes occasionally. You chisel it down but it depends where it is. If it's in the middle, then you take a quarter-inch off the stone and do it again. If you're lucky you can change it – like a 'C' into a 'G'.

Kelly's workshop with letter carvers at work.

Letter carver Ronald Evans tackles the complexity of written Chinese.

Cutting granite is so hard that, before my time, Kelly's employed a man or boy who did nothing else but sharpen up the chisels on a York stone. In 1928, they brought out tungsten carbide and, when a tool got a bit blunt you sent it up to Faulds in Glasgow, together with a shilling, and they sharpened it up and sent it back. Today, you sharpen them yourself. You want about eighteen chisels to cut marble and at least six for cutting granite. New chisels are expensive.

I am a member of the Letter Cutters' Association. When the chaps came back from the 1914-18 war they found they were poorly paid so they founded the Association. We used to meet generally about four times a year at The George in the Strand. Work is bought by the letter. The firm that you work for gets the orders and the inscriptions and charge double the price they pay to the letter carver. Of course, the firm supplies the materials and gold leaf which is dear.

The finest stone is polished granite – it is imperishable and the polish does not come off. People think it needs to be repolished but it doesn't. It's permanent. From the artistic point of view they use slate and other stones such as Portland stone which is very good but tends to absorb moisture and it 'blows'. Marble comes from Italy. It doesn't weather very well – smoke seems to get into it. After ten years, you can scrape it with a chisel to bring it up again. The Italians, under Mussolini, tended to make sure of the work by charging for the raw stone more or less the same price as worked stone. Granite comes from Balmoral in Scotland but the Germans and French called their stone 'Balmoral' which confused.

Kelly's will soon be closing [Ed.: it is now closed and flats built upon the land]. The firm says that with the increase in land values (it was a country lane before they came here and land was cheap) the site will fetch £$\frac{3}{4}$ to £1 million. The interest from that is greater than selling memorials. There's something wrong there. Whose going to do the work? There are no young letter carvers.

They've got machines that do the work and call themselves 'letter cutters'. It must be a dying trade.

David Moffatt
Recorded April 1986

CHAPTER 13
The Butcher's Tale

Bell Lane, Hendon, 1922. The Bell pub is on the left but the adjacent shops, and much else besides, were demolished in the 1970s.

Golders Green station, *c*. 1907. As can be seen, horse buses were still being used.

I am eighty-seven years of age and was born in Wimborne in Dorset. My mother wished her boys to have a trade. I already had a connection with the trade because we had a farmer's son living with us who had gone into the meat trade, and since the age of ten I had been a 'Saturday boy' when I carried a wooden tray on my shoulders for deliveries for a local butcher. So I have been in the meat trade since I was ten until I retired at eighty-five years of age!

I was apprenticed to learn the trade in Wimborne at 1s 6d a week. I did four years learning to be a real butcher – that is bring the livestock from the market through the streets to the lairage for slaughtering the next day. I killed my first beast with a pole-axe when I was sixteen. Slaughtering in those days was awful. There were no such things as humane killers and they were not even stunned. We just put a knife in.

In 1913, I advertised for a job as a butcher and had a reply from Mr Doe of Hendon who had a shop in Bell Lane, next to the Bell Inn. He hadn't been in business long and was a London-style butcher (he bought his meat in Smithfield Market) not a real butcher. I came up to London by train and was met by Mr Doe at Waterloo and we went on the tube to Golders Green which I remember mystified me. I was paid 10s a week and didn't stay very long. From there I went to West End Lane, Hampstead, where I had a little three-wheeler to drive around – a tricycle – and we did the hotels. I was twenty-two at the time and one day, speaking to a policeman, I mentioned that I would like to get into the meat trade for myself. He said 'There's a shop going in the Burroughs at Hendon.' It was a dairy then, with a nice big window and a nice forecourt with white painted posts and chains. There was no lease and I took it at £2 per week and paid the rates. I bought an ice-box, second hand, for £18 from a firm in Church End, Finchley, and was confident of success because I knew the trade well and was not just a meat salesman.

From this humble beginning I built up a business offering good quality and I was in that first shop for seven years. Hendon was then coming into its own. There was no Hendon Central but the streets had been planned and were ready for houses to be built. As the furniture vans came into the district we would follow them and present to the lady of the house our card and ask to be given a trial. I served a lot of places such as Brampton Grove and the Downage and we eventually had four bikes and a van running round in the 1920s. The boys were paid 30s a week and it cost 7s 6d a week to hire a bike. Business was built on delivery and many of our customers became our friends. Competition was keen. Hendon was a small place. Sainsbury's in Brent Street was my biggest competitor because they sold beautiful meat and cut the price. But the family of Oliver at Church End, Hendon, were very keen. They were five brothers working there and they'd get on their bikes and follow up the furniture vans. It was keen competition – I tell you! Like me, the Olivers were Salvationists and one brother played in my band for years. In fact, when I first came to Hendon, my first invitation to tea, on my first Sunday, was from the Olivers. We were always great friends.

On a typical workday I would get up at 4.30 a.m. and go on the first tube to Smithfield to arrive about 5.30 a.m. with your order book in your hand. You would go around the wholesalers' shops you knew and haggle the price, finally agree it, and a skewer would be put in the meat to mark it with your name. In the early days,

Church End, Hendon, *c*. 1910. The Olivers' butchers shop was in a terrace adjacent to St Mary's parish church and was demolished to make way for the Heritage Centre.

Audley Road, Hendon, in the 1930s. Parked cars are beginning to appear as a regular feature in the streets. There was fierce competition between local traders for the custom of households in streets such as this.

a carrier (horse-drawn) would be booked to take the meat to the van.

I liked to be back in the shop about 7.30 a.m. after having a piece of toast and coffee at the market. We would then put up a 'nice front' – that is, dress the window with say ten lambs and various cuts of meat. Then we made up orders from customers which might have been taken the previous day. Rump steak was about 2s 6d per pound: cheaper cuts such as flank of beef was about $3\frac{1}{2}$d per pound. Orders were put into a book. In some cases, the cook or housekeeper would order but generally it would be the lady of the house. Even in places like Audley Road, for example, most people had a servant.

During the week, we would close at six or seven o'clock and about eight or nine o'clock on Friday and Saturday. In fact, in the early days, we would go on to ten o'clock on a Saturday. The shop was cleaned at midday and at night with a really thorough clean at the weekend. Christmas, for example, was a great burden. We would go to market but it was such a muddle – the poultry was just pushed into big heaps and finding the weight you wanted was like finding a needle in a haystack. Families were larger then and would want a bigger bird. They were already plucked but we would have to dress them.

I think the way people buy their meat today is much more attractive than years ago. The presentation and packing is good.

Fred Cobb
Recorded February 1981

71

CHAPTER 14
The Farmer's Tale

Mrs Yeaxlee with one of the classes at St James's School, Friern Barnet Lane. She was the wife of the headmaster and they lived in a small cottage at the back of the school.

Albert Street School taught woodwork and other practical subjects both to its own pupils and to visiting children from other schools.

I was born on 20 January 1907 at 11 Friern Place, Oakleigh Road, Whetsone. Both my mother's and father's side were in farming. My grandfather was born in Yorkshire and when he came down this way he took over Brook Farm in Whetstone in 1890 or so. He also became the licensee of the Black Bull (then known as the Bull) and did both jobs.

I went to school at St James's, Friern Barnet Lane, but I fell out with the headmaster, Mr Yeaxlee. The trouble was that we had an old collie sheepdog that absolutely stank. The dog thought the world of me and would follow me to school and go beneath the desk. One day, the headmaster went to hit me and I butted him with my head and knocked him into the fire. I was transferred to Albert Street School, Finchley, where I never looked back.

I left school at fourteen and went to work on my uncle's farm, Floyd Dairy, which was where the Whetstone police station now stands and where I was brought up. When I was six years of age I milked four cows by hand before I went to school and four more when I had finished. When my uncle went into hospital during the 1914-18 war, when I was six or so, I even ran the farm which was about 50 acres. We had land in Friern Barnet Lane where Queenswell School now stands: we had 35 acres in Oakleigh Park and plots down Oakleigh Road and Oakleigh Park North.

We kept a dozen pigs or so at a time and killed a pig every week which we sold to people who called at the farm. The carcass would be put into a copper of boiling water, scalded and scraped with a 'scud' to cleanse the hair off. You can see a scud in Barnet Museum marked 'believed to be a flour scoop'!

Harry Broadbelt on his uncle's farm in Friern Barnet Lane. Today's police station stands on the site.

Brook Farm, Whetstone, in 1914, just before its demolition.

My uncle paid me about £2 a week. I used to get up at 6 a.m., hand-milk the cows and take them down to one of the fields by driving them along the roads. The milk was put into a cooler and then into churns. Our water came from a pump and the well never ran dry. The temperature of the water was just the reverse of the weather outside. On a very cold day it came out steaming and on a really hot day, was icy cold. I cannot offer an explanation for this. The crude way my uncle had of stopping the pump from freezing up was, every week, to throw a barrow load of manure round the base of the pump.

We barely made a living. There was a kitchen garden so we never bought vegetables; fruit trees and we kept poultry (selling the eggs) and a few turkeys. Down Oakleigh Park there was a spinney full of rabbits and we did a lot of rabbiting with ferrets.

My uncle, George Floyd, was an old bachelor and the meanest man who ever lived! He always kept his money in a wallet and nobody ever saw what he had in that wallet. When he brought it out to pay anyone, he turned his back on them!

I left the farm to go into the Army in 1922 and when I came out in 1925 my uncle offered me the dairy business. Within six months I had built a good dairy round with no end of trade. I started off with a motorcycle combination on to which I built a long sidecar to take the cans and bottles. Eventually I built up two rounds and employed a couple of chaps but we had to buy in the milk. They used horse-drawn carts and the bottles were of a wide-neck type with a cardboard stopper.

After the sale of Floyd's Farm to United Dairies, Harry Broadbelt became a round inspector for the company.

I did seven yeas of hard labour when I took over that business in 1925! I started at 5.30 a.m. and was still going at ten o'clock at night. The only day I ever had off was to travel to Durham to get married and I returned the next night. We went to the pictures twice during the seven years and on both occasions I fell asleep! I couldn't even sit down to have my dinner without falling asleep.

In 1933, we sold out to the Manor Farm Dairy of Finchley – now the United Dairies. They offered us a good price – I think it was £18 a gallon. [Ed.: That is, they were compensated for every gallon of milk that they delivered on their rounds]. We were doing 128 gallons a day and the deal tied us down so that we could not sell milk within a three-mile radius of the farm and therefore couldn't start up against them.

They took me on as a round inspector. Knowing the trade I was a handy chap for them and I checked up on a different round every day. The Totteridge round was the best round for 'fiddles' in the whole depot. The big houses never kept accounts of what they had: put down $\frac{1}{2}$lb of butter that they never had and that was $\frac{1}{2}$lb in your pocket. What you could fiddle was called 'sparrers'.

The sale broke my uncle up. He had nothing to do. One day, I think it was in 1935, I was having my breakfast when my brother-in-law came running down and said 'Uncle George has committed suicide'. I ran out and cut him down but he was cold and had been there for some time.

Harry Broadbelt
Recorded January 1981

CHAPTER 15

The Coal Merchant's Tale

Daniel's Almshouses, Hendon, *c.* 1910.

Schweppes' horse-drawn transport was a feature in the roads of West Hendon where the factory was located.

I was born in 1915 at No. 9 The Burroughs, Hendon. My father and mother were both Hendonians and lived in Heading Street and Ravenshurst Avenue. My grandfather and grandmother were also Hendonians but I only vaguely remember my grandmother who used to live in the almshouses in the Burroughs. On Sunday, as it came your turn, you would take the Sunday dinner up to her. My father, who died in 1932, was a printer. He was the first linotype operator on the *Hendon & Finchley Times* when Mr Warden was the owner and was there all his working life.

We had a neighbour called Tom Rowland who ran the farrier's shop and shod the horses for Schweppes. We got very friendly and, as a child, I used to go round with him on the horse and cart because he also ran a coal delivery business. The farrier's shop was in decline so he started a coal business in 1928/29 and in 1932 opened a coal office in Station Road, Hendon and I started with him.

Down at the Hendon LMS station there were about six coal merchants. Each one bought coal through factors in the City where you had the Coal Exchange. The factor came round every week and he ordered direct from the collieries on your behalf. Over the years you learned about the characteristics of various coals from the different collieries. The main coal was house-coal for the open fires which came from Notts. It would come to Hendon station where we had our siding and I would go and see the shunting clerk and arrange for the wagons to be delivered to our sidings. They delivered each wagon exactly where you wanted it and it was wonderful organization. The coal was unloaded by the coalman direct from the open-topped eleven-ton wagons into bags.

Mostly you tried to clear a wagon of, say, anthracite, direct into the bags to go to the customer but what was left over was put into bays for a rainy day. Usually a team of two men unloaded the wagon. They had no special clothing except a leather hood with a leather back but this was unpopular because as you bent over to empty the sack it nearly broke your neck! The coal was loaded into one-hundredweight capacity bags standing on scales called 'dead-weights' and put straight on to the cart. If there was only one man working on his own, the empty sack would be hooked on to an 'iron-man' which stood four feet high. When full of coal you would wind a handle till the sack was shoulder high and then load it on to the cart.

They were all horses and carts then and about two tons would be loaded onto the cart. Generally, the coalman delivered about two loads a day. Some carts used two horses to pull and you

Hendon Central Underground station, c. 1923. The extension of the Northern line to Edgware brought in its wake demands for houses and flats of every description. All used solid fuel for heating.

Cool Oak Lane, Hendon, as it looked in 1910 when housing estates were being developed.

could get more on that way. During snowy weather a tracer-horse was used. This was a horse with a chain from his collar to the leading horse of the wagon and helped to pull them up the hill. They used to screw special studs into the shoes in winter weather. We had our own horses but with the changing times went over to lorries about 1926.

The price of best coal at that time was 1s per hundredweight. Today [1981] it costs about £5. The coal in those days was better. As you know, there were depressed mining areas but this was usually because the coal was of inferior quality. The Government put a quota on the 'better quality' collieries thinking that when this quota was used up it would give the depressed areas a chance for more work. But it didn't work that way. No one wanted inferior quality coal so the merchants would wait until the next month's quota came

along: so it didn't do the trade any good at all. Not only that, the better quality collieries, when they sold their quota, were also out of work.

Coal sacks, as I remember, came from an old firm called A.R. Webster in Stepney. They were made from the best hessian to withstand the terrific strain. A sack cost about a guinea and they didn't have a long life – not because they wore out but because many were lost from the lorries. A lost sack could mean the loss of profit for one day's work.

In those early days we sold about ten tons a week but we finished up with 5,000 customers and five lorries going. This area (Hendon) was being built up so you couldn't go wrong. Vivian Avenue, Hendon Central and round that way all wanted solid fuel until after the last war when oil came in. A 'coaly' working his guts out got paid about thirty bob a week. He worked from morn till dusk, starting at 7 a.m. and finishing when the job was done around 6 p.m. Even up to the war [1939] a man doing a ten-ton load picked up about £3 10s a week.

It's a funny thing that once in the trade they rarely leave it. It's the cleanest dirt there is, as any doctor will tell you. If a coalman cuts his finger he never puts anything on it. The iodine in the coal does all that and he rarely gets poison in the cut. Another thing: you go home, wash and it all comes off! There's something about the coal trade, I don't know what, but it's a clean way of getting dirty.

Len Warner
Recorded January 1981

CHAPTER 16

The Stage Manager's Tale

The Golders Green Hippodrome opened on 26 December 1913. It was originally a music hall but, from the early 1920s until its closure in 1968, it staged plays, operas, ballets and orchestral concerts. Many famous artistes trod its boards. It is used today by the BBC as a recording studio.

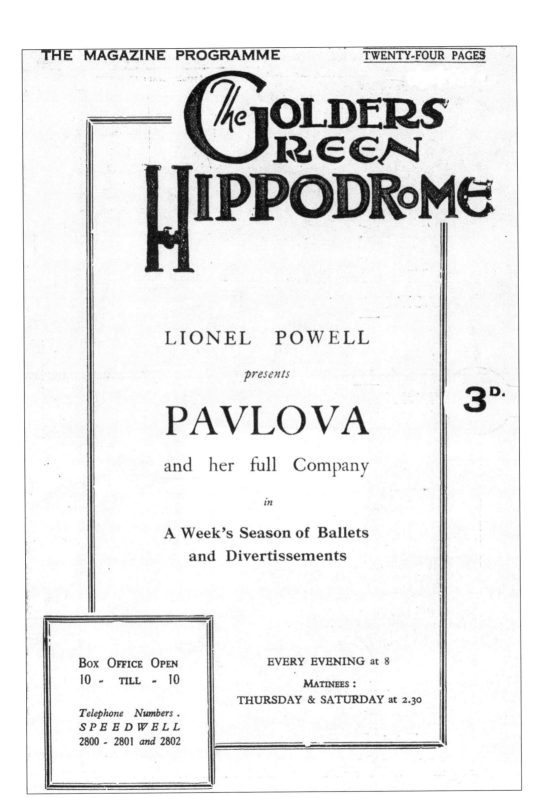

The GOLDERS GREEN HIPPODROME

LIONEL POWELL

presents

PAVLOVA

and her full Company

in

A Week's Season of Ballets and Divertissements

3D.

BOX OFFICE OPEN
10 - TILL - 10

Telephone Numbers .
S P E E D W E L L
2800 - 2801 *and* 2802

EVERY EVENING at 8

MATINEES :
THURSDAY & SATURDAY at 2.30

A programme for the performance of the great ballerina Anna Pavlova on 8 December 1930.

The splendid service offered by the trams, with their early start and late finish, encouraged theatre-going and was a particular boon to those working late at the theatre. The Hippodrome tram stop was outside the nearby Underground station.

I was born on 26 December 1896 at Old Street in the City. In 1898, my father bought some local shops and cottages in Summers Lane, Finchley, and we moved to Finchley where I went to Albert Street School. I left school in 1910.

I remember Finchley when it was Finchley! It was practically all fields and there was a racecourse at Granville Road and Kingsway where you could do your courting. They took down the rails after they built the tram station.

I was unemployed after the First World War and used to go to see 'Father Feed 'em All' [the Relieving Officer]. A job was going at Golders Green Hippodrome and when I got to the theatre, Nobby Clark, the stage door keeper, gave me directions where to go to get on the stage. There was only a

tiny beam of light on that big stage and I don't mind admitting that I had the 'wind up' and was going to leave when suddenly the lights went up and it looked better! The stage manager Mr Dyer saw me and I got paid 4s a night and 3s 6d for matinées, i.e. 31s a week.

I knew nothing about the stage. The Hippodrome had a different play every week except when you got a season of grand opera or light opera – the D'Oyly Carte, for example. Sometimes, when there was a long first act, you could sit and watch the play. I used to do a bit of prompting for which I got paid 4s a night extra. The actors sometimes left out whole pages – it depended on what they had to drink!

I worked twice on the stage with Charles Laughton. First time was a walk-on part in *Payment Deferred* when I played the part of Sergeant Higgins of Scotland Yard in which Laughton dislocated my thumb in a 'fight'. I then had a speaking part in *On the Spot* in 1932 where Charles Laughton played a Chicago gangster. In the play he shoots me (and I'm going to quote you a line from the play) and when I'm lying on the carpet with blood coming from six bullet wounds, he says, 'Don't spoil my carpet, you bastard!' and puts two more shots into me! I don't think the audience minded the bad language because that's how Chicago gangsters were expected to talk.

One play that sticks in my mind was *Silver Wings* with Harry Welchman which was about flying in the First World War. Here we had an actual plane suspended by fine wires which 'crashes' on the stage, killing the pilot. On the special effects side, a big metal sheet would be lowered from the flies which was rattled to produce thunder; 'rain' was a box with wires in it and stones that rolled around inside and horses were done by coconut shells.

The audiences were very large, especially when Gracie Fields was playing. Other artists who pulled them in were Jessie Matthews, Evelyn Laye, Gertrude Lawrence and Jack Buchanan. I also remember Madame Pavlova who used to be most generous. Every night she gave each of the boys half a crown for a drink. I loved the ballet and used to put up the scenery for her Dying Swan.

I've got a little story about Gracie Fields. At one matinée she said to me, 'Come here a moment and pull back the stage curtain a bit. Can you see that parson [sic] down there in the fauteuils? You know my song *Sally*, you watch when I bring out the word "Cor Blimey". I'm going to emphasize it and you'll see that parson get up and walk out.' Which he did! He walked out disgusted.

We used to start work at 9 a.m. and I would get a 2d fare on the open-decked tram from Finchley to Golders Green. On a typical Monday, there might be a scene-rehearsal in the morning where you start with the last scene and work back to the first scene which you left up for the performance. Golders Green had the record for quick changes. When the final curtain came down, we would strike the last act scenery, have a fag and finish about 11.15 p.m. We would go home on a late tram, call in at Bob's coffee-stall in Finchley for tea and a wad, and then go home.

When I got on a bit I worked long hours but would take home on average £10 a week, which was a lot of money. But, if you want to be on the stage, you've got to drink and mix with the artists. In 1934, I got the sack. I had been drinking and blotted my copybook by being drunk and ordering the House Manager off the stage. The biggest single thing that sticks in my mind was that I was a bloody fool to get the sack – I was so happy there. When the 'Hipp' was going to close they sent for us. Many went but I bloody well didn't go! And there was £10 for me! Everyone who had ever worked there was called back and given a bit of a 'do' on the stage.

Joe Howe
Recorded April 1981

CHAPTER 17
The Schoolboy's Tale

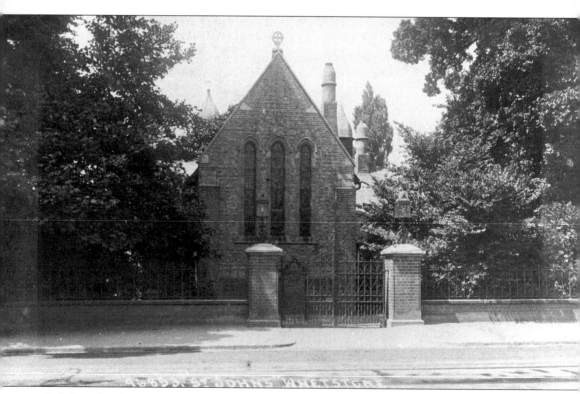

St John's church, Whetstone, was consecrated on 9 May 1832. It stands on land donated by local philanthropist and businessman Joseph Baxendale who also played a major role in the formation of St John's School.

A class at St John's School, *c*. 1920. The school, originally in Totteridge Lane, moved to Britannia Road in 1863 and was relocated to its present site in Swan Lane in the 1970s.

I started at St John's School, Britannia Road, Finchley, in 1908 when I was four years old. Mr Mellor taught Standard 4. He was a real gentleman and we had a little rhyme about him which we used to say, not for him to hear and with no disrespect to him, which went:

Mr Mellor is a very good man,
He tries to teach us all he can;
Reading, writing, arithmetic,
He never forgets to give us the stick.
When he does it makes us dance
Out of England into France;
Out of France and into Spain,
Over the hills and back again.

His wife and son were also teachers at the school.

There was an open fireplace in Standard 4 and going into the room early one morning I found a piece of coal had fallen out and the floorboards in front of the hearth was on fire. I got some water and put out the fire. When Mr Mellor came in, he thanked me and gave me a few coppers. Another time I helped carry in two boys who had broken their legs. When Mr Mellor died, several of us in his class went to the cemetery and a plaque was unveiled to him over the fireplace in his classroom.

Crime and Punishment

I was never in Mr Berry's class but I did get the cane from him for swinging on the gate. I also remember, when we used to kick a tennis ball about in playtime, we picked sides and Bill Day, who was having his pick, said 'I'll have Ginger'. Now Mr Berry was a red-head and he heard Bill who was sent in for the cane.

Friday afternoon was rather easy: Mrs Cowling would read us a chapter of *Treasure Island*. One afternoon, when she went out of the room, several of us started throwing a sponge about which went out of the window. When Mrs Cowling came back she had the sponge in her hand and some of the girls told her how it had come to be outside. Four of us got four cuts each with the cane. It was quite something listening to sixteen cuts but how the third and fourth hurt!

Lighter Moments

We had a girl in our class called Kitty Matthews who could play the piano so she was the pianist for singing lessons. We learned the Russian and the Belgian national anthems. The latter was in French and I don't know whether we had the right words because we learned them parrot fashion.

The 93rd North London (St John's) Scout troop, *c*. 1915. The troop was one of the most popular in the area and had its own band whose instruments had been bought from the proceeds of money earned by the boys at concerts in Woodside Hall.

We had a troop of Boy Scouts, the 93rd North London, connected with the school and St John's church, Whetstone. We would drill in the playground and on Sundays paraded in the school and marched to the church where Mr Keymour was vicar and Mr Swain the choirmaster. We gave a concert in the Woodside Hall, the proceeds going to pay for a drum and bugle band and a trek-cart.

We children were sometimes asked to go to Woodlands in Whetstone High Road (which was a film studio) to act in school scenes. This was usually on a Saturday. We we were given lunch and a sixpence as were there all day. One of the films was *The Girl of My Heart* and it was shown in the Finchley Rink cinema. George Moore Marriott was caretaker there and he was to become famous as the old man in Will Hay's comedies.

We had outings at school. We went to the zoo and different museums by Tube – the first time for most of us and also used a lift for the first time. We also went to Folly Farm in one of Alf Cook's hay carts driven by Mr Main, to Hadley Woods and to the Palace Tea Gardens where we were entertained by a conjurer.

Jack Prime
Recorded June 1978

CHAPTER 18

The Nursery School Pioneer's Tale

Beatrix Tudor-Hart who founded Fortis Green School.

In fine weather, classes at Fortis Green were held in the school's large garden.

Imaginative and creative play was encouraged at Fortis Green School.

I was born in Paris in 1903. My father was an artist who had been turned out of home because his father disapproved of artists and he had come to stay in Paris where he worked at the Beaux Arts. My mother was a marvellously progressive woman, energetic and very much in advance of her time. We were never punished as children, or shouted at, and she gave us plenty of opportunities for doing and discovering things on our own.

I went to a Froebel kindergarten in Paris at the age of four and at seven went to a school called *L'Ecole Ancienne*, considered the most progressive school in France. We left France for England in 1913 because the French government said my father should become naturalized if he intended to stay. My parents decided not to change their nationality and we came to Hampstead which at first I hated. I was sent to the South Hampstead High School for Girls at which I took an examination so that they could place me. I was doing the French paper which, being French, I did in a few minutes and started to look round at the other girls. The invigilating teacher suddenly shouted at me 'Stop cheating'. At that moment I hated her, the school and the other children who were staring at me. I was very unhappy at the school because the girls said I was a 'Frenchy'.

I passed the entrance exam for Newnham College, Cambridge, in 1922. I found myself in a completely different world from my home which I had come to dislike because my mother, whom I adored, had died and my father had remarried. My stepmother's ambition was that I should be presented at Court and married off. At Cambridge, I met youngsters who were fighting against the ideas and values of their parents. People were talking about the Russian revolution and its effects on the people in England. For example, there had been a miners' lockout in 1918 and I had reacted to that because the miners' wives and families had nothing.

The tuition at Cambridge was good. I started with French but during my first year I began to read books about psychology. Gestalt psychology was just beginning to be talked about and I decided to take Part II in psychology. I read my first Piaget book in my last year at Cambridge and was very much influenced by him. The Russian Pavlov was also being talked about but it seemed to me not to explain anything whereas Freud was useful.

My thoughts were being turned towards the education of children and how they could be better treated. It was a time of changing values. I graduated in 1925 with a First Class Honours degree and was thus eligible for a research scholarship. I went to the Principal and asked for a research grant. She told me that it was impossible because psychology was not something that could be researched into!

I wrote to Charlotte Bühler (who became famous) who was living in Vienna and asked if I could come to Vienna to do some research work for her. She agreed. It was interesting work. She asked me to do an experiment on how babies learn to recognize the human voice and react differently from when they heard ordinary sounds. To my surprise, I found it took some children only one month of life to change their behaviour when they heard a human voice.

Charlotte Bühler was pleased with the results. She had two children of her own and when I visited them at home I found to my great surprise and shock that they were being brought up in a traditional Prussian way. They were silent: the girl greeted me with a curtsey and the boy with a bending of the knees. Her work had clearly shown children's need for freedom to express themselves and yet she was bringing up her children in the old-fashioned way.

Attitudes in the Twenties

At the end of July '26 I returned to Britain which I found was settling back to accepting the pre-war status quo. I was questioning the way people behaved towards each other socially and I was querying the role of industry, of the master/servant relationship and conditions of living. Then came the General Strike and people everywhere were grumbling. People were underpaid, ill-treated and the rich were behaving very badly. All my family were rich and I met rich people whom I disliked. They were not interested in human beings, happiness and good living conditions.

America

I went to America in August 1926 on a Research Fellowship to Smith College, Massachusetts, for a year to do post-graduate teacher-training and experiments at their Gestalt nursery school. My impressions of those times are vague because we were very much kept in at the college and discouraged from meeting people from the outside.

The college and its teaching was very good. The nursery school was for the children of teachers and was in advance of the Montessori schools I had seen in Vienna. Children had more freedom, were happy, and always had good treatment from the teachers.

The college was close to Boston and it so happened that the famous Saccho and Vanzetti case was being tried at the time. There was a meeting in our town to debate the case and several students and myself decided to go and hear what it was about. The 'prosecutor' finished his speech by saying 'It does not matter whether Saccho and Vanzetti are guilty or not – they are Anarchists and deserve to die'. Whereupon there was violent hissing and clapping and fighting. Police were called in to clear the hall. That experience began to make me think in terms of politics and how politics might or might not play a part in the way people behaved towards one another.

Hampstead Again

In 1928, I decided I wanted to be in a state nursery school helping to develop nursery education. I wrote to Sir Percy Nunn, Director of Education at the LCC, and went to see him. I told him about my qualifications and experience. He said it was not appropriate and I would have to do a Teacher Training Course on Primary Schooling. I asked if this would include nursery work. 'No', he said, 'we are not yet training nursery teachers because we have not enough nursery schools!' I therefore decided to start my own school in Hampstead.

To my surprise, I got twelve pupils straight away. My objectives were to make the children sociable; stop them quarrelling and fighting; to make them get to know other children and how to work and play together. The school grew in size and in 1932 I took another larger house in Hampstead for forty pupils and three teachers. The only sad thing in what were otherwise years of achievement, was that a neighbour, very conventional, disapproved of our nursery school and finally brought a court action against us. Susan Isaacs spoke in our defence. For me, she was the greatest person in England on child behaviour and I think she is still the greatest child behaviourist we have had.

In the courtroom she pointed out that children needed to be properly treated in order to be civilized; deprived children became badly behaved. The court case, because of widespread reporting, became very famous – partly because this had never happened before to a nursery school. The judge, in the end, had to deny that the school was incorrectly conducted. It was proved to be well run but he found the garden was too small and the school therefore a nuisance to neighbours. I had to pay costs. The

owner of the house wrote to the local papers a few weeks after the case to say that it was hard lines for a man who wanted to sell his house to have a school next to it!

The Hunger Marches

During the Depression I saw people begging in the streets, something I had never seen before – even in France of the early 1900s. I remember the hunger marchers marching across Hampstead and I joined them. I listened to the speeches and I boarded some of the marchers in my home because they had nowhere to sleep. The Hampstead population didn't seem to bother at all – they were too pre-occupied with their own problems. The marchers were not just Communists but ordinary people who came from different parts of the country. They were very bitter and angry at the Government's failure to stimulate the economy and give people adequate money to live on.

A New School

In 1936, we placed an advertisement in the New Statesman saying we were thinking of starting a progressive school and would anyone interested come to a meeting at a local hall. More than 100 people came to the meeting and we discussed a school consciously run on socialist, co-operative lines – a co-operative, that is, of parents and teachers. There would be no head but an elected committee of teachers and parents to run the school. To our surprise, we got enough support to start a new school.

The appalling conditions of those times meant that many large houses were for sale, very cheap. Finally, in 1936, we were lucky enough to find a block of four houses standing in $1\frac{1}{4}$ acres of ground in Fortis Green, East Finchley. By 1938, the school was running with thirty children – mostly nursery – but some aged up to ten years. As far as I am aware, it was the first progressive day-school to be founded.

Beatrix Tudor-Hart
Recorded July 1979